WHAT KIND OF FRIEND ARE YOU?

By Brooke Rowe

45th Parallel Press

Published in the United States of America by Cherry Lake Publishing
Ann Arbor, Michigan
www.cherrylakepublishing.com

Reading Adviser: Marla Conn, ReadAbility, Inc.
Book Designer: Melinda Millward

Photo Credits: © William Perugini/Shutterstock.com, back cover, 4; © monkeybusinessimages/Thinkstock.com, back cover, 4; © Rick Becker-Leckrone/Shutterstock Images, cover, 1, 31; © Monkey Business Images, 6, 30; © Pamela Moore/istockphoto.com, 6; © Ollyy/Shutterstock Images, 7; © Edyta Pawlowska/Shutterstock Images, 7; © Pramecomix/Shutterstock Images, 8; © Photodisc/Thinkstock.com, 8; © BestPhotoStudio/Shutterstock Images, 9; © g-stockstudio/Thinkstock.com, 9; © iofoto/Shutterstock Images, 10, 18; © Karramba Production/Shutterstock Images, 10; © SolStock/Shutterstock Images, 11; © Aaron Amat/Shutterstock Images, 11; ©Miss Wetzel's Art Class /http://www.flickr.com/CC-BY-SA 2.0, 12; © YanLev/Thinkstock.com, 12; © monkeybusinessimages/Thinkstock.com, 13; © adrian825/Thinkstock.com, 13; © muzsy / Shutterstock.com, 14; © Ingram Publishing/Thinkstock.com, 14, 21; © Michael Chamberlin/Shutterstock Images, 15; © lazyllama/Shutterstock Images, 15; © oliveromg/Shutterstock Images, 16; © Syda Productions/Shutterstock Images, 16, 17; © Stockbyte/Thinkstock.com, 17; © Hemera Technologies/Thinkstock.com, 18; © Ariwasabi/Shutterstock Images, 19; © Alexander Kirch/Shutterstock Images, 19; © Rawpixel/Shutterstock Images, 20; © Feverpitched/Thinkstock.com, 20; © Sabphoto/Shutterstock Images, 21; © CREATISTA/Shutterstock Images, 22, 30; © rmnoa357/Shutterstock Images, 22; © digitalskillet/Thinkstock.com, 23; © ASIFE/Thinkstock.com, 23; © Prixel Creative/Shutterstock Images, 24; © wavebreakmedia/Shutterstock Images, 24; © Konstantin Chagin/Shutterstock Images, 25; © Jupiterimages/Thinkstock.com, 25; © Carrienelson1 | Dreamstime.com - Jaden Smith, Willow Smith Photo, 26; © Featureflash | Dreamstime.com - Daniel Radcliffe, Emma Watson, Rupert Grint Photo, 26; © Photo Works / Shutterstock.com, 27; © violetblue/Shutterstock Images, 27; © Rob Mattingley/istockphoto.com, 28; © racorn/Shutterstock Images, 28; © ArminStautBerlin/Thinkstock.com, 29; © Elena Elisseeva/Thinkstock.com, 29; © LuckyBusiness/Thinkstock.com, 31

Graphic Element Credits: © Silhouette Lover/Shutterstock Images, back cover, multiple interior pages; © Arevik/Shutterstock Images, back cover, multiple interior pages; © tukkki/Shutterstock Images, multiple interior pages; © paprika/Shutterstock Images, 24

45th Parallel Press is an imprint of Cherry Lake Publishing.

Library of Congress Cataloging-in-Publication Data

Rowe, Brooke.
   What kind of friend are you? / Brooke Rowe.
pages cm. — (Best quiz ever)
Includes index.
ISBN 978-1-63470-039-9 (hardcover) — ISBN 978-1-63470-093-1 (pdf) —
ISBN 978-1-63470-066-5 (pbk.) — ISBN 978-1-63470-120-4 (ebook)
1. Friendship—Miscellanea—Juvenile literature. 2. Personality tests—Juvenile literature. I. Title.

BF575.F66R69 2016
155.2'83—dc23   2015009916

Table of Contents

Introduction

Hey! Welcome to the Best Quiz Ever series. This is a book. Duh. But it's also a pretty awesome quiz. Don't worry. It's not about math. Or history. Or anything you might get graded on. Snooze.

This is a quiz all about YOU.

To Take the Best Quiz Ever:

Answer honestly!
Keep track of your answers. But don't write in the book!
(Hint: Make a copy of this handy chart.)
Don't see the answer you want? Pick the closest one.
Take it alone. Take it with friends!
Have fun! Obviously.

Question 1 _____   Question 7 _____

Question 2 _____   Question 8 _____

Question 3 _____   Question 9 _____

Question 4 _____   Question 10 _____

Question 5 _____   Question 11 _____

Question 6 _____   Question 12 _____

To get a copy of this activity, visit
www.cherrylakepublishing.com/activities.

Your perfect locker partner would be:

A. To have my own!

B. My BFF

C. This year's "new kid"

D. Uh ... no idea ...

Did you know?

BFF is used in texting. It means Best Friend Forever.

Your rapper name would be:

A. Zesty Cobra

B. Power Flash

C. Sunshine Sugar

D. Wicked **Whisper**

Did you know?

In 2014, a pet white cobra escaped and **roamed** its neighborhood for many days before it was caught. It now lives in the San Diego Zoo.

Your dad offers to drive you and your friends to the movies to see the latest blockbuster. You say:

A. Nah, I'd rather see it alone

B. Great! I'll call Ben and Amy!

C. Just drop me off.
I'll see who's there!

D. My friends already
saw it without me

Did you know?
The book 1000 Awesome Things *ranks*
"Going to the Movies Alone" number 398.

It's your birthday! How do you celebrate?

A. My best friend sends me a message online

B. My friends decorate my locker

C. I bring cupcakes for everyone

D. Normal day, thank goodness!

Did you know?

Have you ever gotten cash from an **ATM**? The Sprinkles Cupcake ATMs sell cupcakes from an automated machine.

What's your favorite position on the soccer team?

A. Goalie

B. Center forward

C. Wherever the coach puts me!

D. Benchwarmer/ cheerleader

Did you know?
The 2014 FIFA World Cup in Brazil made $4 billion.

You're moving to a new school. What's going to be the best part?

A. Leaving everyone at my old school

B. Being the awesome "new kid"

C. Meeting lots of new people

D. Being unnoticed on the first day

Did you know?

The boy band New Kids on the Block got together in 1984, broke up in 1994, and got back together in 2008.

It's Career Day at school! Which presentation are you most excited to see?

A. The zookeeper

B. The supermodel

C. The filmmaker

D. Whichever. Just don't bring me onstage.

Did you know?
Stage fright has happened to singers Adele, Jackie Evancho, Lorde, and Niall Horan.

It's 2050 and you're president. You get a call that we're about to enter World War III. What do you do?

A. Whatever my gut tells me

B. Whatever is best for Americans

C. Whatever it takes to bring peace

D. Quit ASAP, then hide under my favorite blanket

Did you know?

The **assassination** of Archduke Franz Ferdinand started World War I.

Where are you in your family's birth order?

A. Only child

B. Oldest

C. Youngest

D. Middle

Did you know?

Families with only one child have almost doubled in number since the 1960s.

Which of these school activities would you NEVER join?

A. A team sport

B. Tutoring other kids after school

24

C. What do you mean?
I'll join anything!

D. Drama Club

Did you know?

About five out of 1,000 high school
baseball players have a chance of
playing in the majors.

Who would be your first choice to play you in a movie?

A. Emma Watson or Daniel Radcliffe

B. Willow Smith or Jaden Smith

26

C. Bella Thorne or Adam Irigoyen

D. Why would I want a movie made about me?

Did you know?
Daniel Radcliffe was paid 80 times more to play Harry Potter in the last movie than he was in the first.

The new kid asks you to get ice cream after school. What do you say?

A. Thanks, but I've got other plans

B. Sorry! I have to run to the pep rally!

28

C. Sounds great! What's your name again?

D. Uh ... well ... I ... uh ...

Did you know?

The Dairy Queen Blizzard was introduced in 1985.
More than 175 million Blizzards were sold that year.

You're done! Now you tally your score. Add up your As, Bs, Cs, and Ds. What letter do you have the most of? BTW, if you have a tie, you're a little bit of both.

As: Lone Wolf

You like to do your own thing! You don't need tons of friends. The friends you do have are good ones. And that's what counts. You're confident enough to check out fun stuff on your own. No posse needed. Being independent is great. But don't be afraid to talk to other people a little more often.

Bs: Mr./Miss Popularity

You're in high demand! People look up to you and are always trying to join your crowd. But you prefer hanging out with your friends. Only. Tagalongs need not apply. Try branching out a little more! And you might be surprised how fun a Saturday alone can be.

Cs: Social Butterfly

You might not be one of the "cool kids." But the good thing is, everyone likes having you around. You're friendly and easy to get along with. You can hang out with anyone you like! You don't care about social status. You make friends with whomever you want. And people like that about you.

Ds: Wallflower

You hate being in the spotlight! You'd rather do stuff on your own than with people you don't know. Sometimes you get a little nervous about talking to new people. But that will get easier. And if you come across another wallflower? You might be able to bring down each other's walls. Sometimes the best friends are the ones you never expected.

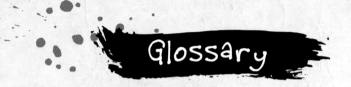

Glossary

assassination (uh-SAS-uh-nay-shun) the killing of someone who is well-known or important

ATM a machine linked to a bank that lets you put money into your account or take it out without visiting the bank

roam (rohm) to wander without purpose or plan

tutor (TOO-tuhr) a teacher who gives private lessons

whisper (WIS-pur) a soft sound

Index